Hospice

Winner of the 2024 New Women's Voice Series

poems by

Molly Akin

Finishing Line Press
Georgetown, Kentucky

Hospice

New Women's Voices Series, No. 186

ACKNOWLEDGMENTS

Thank you to the following publications for publishing earlier versions of
these poems:

"River Bottom"—Honorable Mention, Tulip Tree Publishing *Wild Woman*
"Mothering is a social construct, and I am motherless" *Inflectionist Review*
"Executor of Tangible Goods" *Identity Theory*

Publisher: Leah Huete de Maines
Editor: Christen Kincaid
Cover Art: Molly Akin
Author Photo: Heather Grey
Cover Design: Elizabeth Maines McCleavy

Order online: www.finishinglinepress.com
also available on amazon.com and bookshop.org

Author inquiries and mail orders:
Finishing Line Press
PO Box 1626
Georgetown, Kentucky 40324
USA

Contents

To my family, teachers, and friends.
Most especially my husband, Joe,
for being my first reader and most trusted sounding board.

Ladybug

"Hospice" comes from the Latin hospitem "guest, stranger, sojourner, visitor" also "host; one bound by ties of hospitality—traveler's rest"

It's not just ladybugs

slow dragging wings
seeping out of curves
under red burnished shells

Every winter they come

A bumblebee calling
out a final walk

a rabbit curled under a bush
its white poof
the last to decay

I wonder if it's true
they only come here
to die

Mice and toads
in window wells

katydids singing in my garage
after the first hard freeze

My mother comes
close now

with her aphid brow
and bone cradled cancers

more metastasis than mother

Mothering is a social construct, and I am motherless

There is
no mother

a fresh
bell ring

perhaps
there was

never

      "*Mother*"

now
absence
is definite

absence

an old
bell rung

Tail

I see my mother's tail
bone

wrapped together
in loose arrangement
bones

my mother's tail
curls
bone

my mother sits
on her tail
tucked
between
bone

my mother's bone
sits on her tail

on top of bone

her bone
grinds

her bones
now ground

her bones
poured into
ground

I saw

my mother's tail

Scan

A worm goes searching for something undisturbed and dark. A bird goes searching for a worm. The chicks search for the sound of wings. My backyard chickadee searches for predators. A little robotic ticking of head to head. Scan, scan —all safe and pop in. When I wake I cannot locate her. I am no longer waiting for a worm. A worm goes searching for the dark. A bird searches for a worm. I search for my dead mother in the dark of early morning. A little robotic tick tick of *mama*, oh *mama's dead.*

Empty

On the day
before she died
my mother

told me
her thoughts
were empty

thoughts
followed fast
by the rest

the rest
of her
emptied

medical supply
bed
emptied

grief
hollowed
empty

My grief stays young

As I became round
And full and gave birth

My mother became round
With tumors

*

My grief stays young

*

I hold it close
Letting it rest in comfort

*

My grief has fangs

*

I bring its soft muzzle
Delicate pink mouth
To my feeding breast

*

It sits at my other breast
As my child weens

*

My grief remains
Mother's fullness returns

*

My grief twitches
Jumps down with new legs

*

My grief is gone

*

My milk
Unheeded as it drips

*

Replaced with
The hollowness

Of slow death

*

My grief turns
Back to me
Becoming young again

If Flowers Speak, or Victorian lore in a dead poet's room

My Emily sits
At the window
Of my mind

Tapping on the
Gentle distortion

Hard won
In the chaos

What do the
Climbing and entwined
Roses have to say

As they curl and grow
Forever watching
Her deathbed

Inheritance

On Monday I woke up and did the laundry. Right away. The basket was barely brimming. I have never done this. My mom looked at me before she died. *What Mama*, I telegraphed blue eye to blue eye. This is it, I guess. *Do your laundry, Molly. I raised you to be diligent.* One of the small rebellions. Letting my laundry pile. Overlooking a tightly wound washcloth until it forms a fetid fold in my nice dress. Now I wake early to wash, dry and fold. A latent power. Efficient domesticity. I am flawless in my grief.

Marked

My mother is buried in an unmarked grave

It is not what it seems
but then I don't know your orientation
towards unmarked graves

I tend to think of history

She would not allow
a marker
only ashed anonymity

Her favorite activity
was to walk
in large black sunglasses

If you ask the attendant they will give a map
a key to unmarked plots

Mother Hunger

She will hunger
From her dry wells
Dry wells and
Bare cupboards

She hungers
Pulling up her
Dry well bucket
Gnawing at health
Until she sees

Bone
Rubbing on bone
Mother hungers
Compares her body
With what was

Wheeled out
Of the operating room

Stripped
reproduction and tumor

She crows her beauty
aged ballerina!

She is dry
And filled with sachets
Of slimming tea

River Bottom

My grandmother is a river
a river bottom woman
soft breasts and wide skirts
smelling of silt and sun.

I remember my grandmother
like the alchemy of the gulf
the Missouri and the Mississippi
pouring her life into mine.

Because my mother drew
from dry wells it is my father's
mother who teaches me
to trace a path in water.

Where muddy waters
spill into lightly salted ocean
our two stories converge
both gone from home at sixteen.

My grandmother and her quilt
hand-sewn by her mother
who poured her body
into scraps of fabric.

I keep her quilt on my bedroom chair
each piece careworn
passed from hand to hand
until its star pattern mirrors the sky.

I dream of my grandmother
and the keening cry of a bird
growing louder until it bursts
washing us in waters no dam can hold.

We carry our sorrows
in these fragile vessels
between wide hips
and river-soaked clothes.

My grandmother taught me
to become a river.

Double Image

I am freed

no longer
of my mother's

body

image—

it took her
death

to wrest
my self

from
her—

her body

slim
no space

for these
thighs—

now I
shake

my flesh

coiled
Siren

Things that cannot be compared

After Sei Shōnagon, Things That Cannot Be Compared,
The Pillow Book

The day of birth is distinct. Like a laugh. Like a cough. Like something slipping high gloss / high cost from a passage too brief.

Three hundred and eighty-five thousand babies born per day.

I birthed two days with my first child and one day with my second. The days of my birthing contained a pushing and a pulling. A vacuum and a long needle.

Any day can contain a laugh, a cough, a push, a pull. Not every day marks you with its passage.

*

In a final death knell, my friend's seventeen-year-old orchid blebbed a baby. She carefully dug it out, separated root stands, and found it a pot. When I heard her mourning, I brought her a new plant. She gifted me her dead plant's child.

The orchid needs constant vigilance to moisture. She will need to dust leaves back to gloss. For it is unable to find a tree to shade under. Its earth stops at her table.

This child is now home with me, where I monitor moisture and soak terracotta in a bowl of water until it is weaned. We want our wild plants to thrive in our homes, but they are uprooted. The best we can do is suspend them temporarily.

Wild plants and house plants appear similar. Colors, shapes, leaf patterns. If you look closely, you will find what cannot be compared. I have plants from deserts and jungles in my shingled coast.

Elephant ears, fringe ferns, orchids, prayer plants, succulents.

This orchid survived the long distance of her travel. Then, it heaved an offspring and shriveled.

Its pot emptied, standing marker to grief.

Voice Memos: My Mother's Cancer

Endometriosis
crawled out
her womb
curling
forward
and back
making
rosettes

More literal
than it sounds

My Mother's Cancer

Spread
up and down
her legs
merging
into cells
spider legs
veinous
marrow
spider pain
leg pain
bone pain
this leg bone
holds pain

My Mother's Cancer

Haunted us
twelve years

Only took
ten days

to deliver
a final
terminal

two doses
of morphine

Cream

I rubbed
my mother's bones
between my hands

her bones
slid skin

she wore
her skin

like ribboning
rivulets

my hands
rubbing

*

remember
how it felt

when young
bones

not thin
bones

she let me
feel useful
this cream
helpful

my touch
soothing

these bones
before incineration

*

now we are
past bones

let me hold
bones

soothe bones
smooth bones

now we
cast bones

away

Executor of tangible goods

My mother's seafoam
table lamp flickers

we invent our hauntings
from feeble connections

Motherhood

Our labors
Interwoven
With contractions
Unspoken

Contracts
Terms of bondage
To systems that refuse
To see our labor

Bonds
Ever pushing and pulling
One big contraction
And it is our life

Looking back
At unceasing demands
On our bodies
In labor

Laboring
For one moment
Of quiet
Before the end

Ten Haikus for 363 Days of Grief

Deathbed bulbs planted
our spent and buried vigil
now open again

I emptied her shelves
my role as a legatee
to suspend and spend

I purchased a horse
inheritance transformed
into living flesh

Mother collected
a shelf full of Plath and Hughes
all spines unbroken

Mother enigma
closely kept her collection
private and pristine

I didn't know her
she kept so many things close
even poetry

I am legatee
inheritor of her goods
shelf heavy with books

I purchased a horse
Sylvia rode Ariel
tepid connection

I'll deadhead the blooms
grief blossoms annually
let it rest again

My grief horse gallops
around the periphery
of understanding

For the year my mother has been dead

Even the troubled mother yearns. By that, I mean I yearn for my troubled mother. Yearn for something untroubled.

I yearn for my mother. By that, I mean I yearn.

I yearn for a different yarn. Something heavy and worsted.

Something I can wrap around the nibbled end of time. A cord to tether my yawning yearning.

By that, I mean I do not want to remember her troubled corpse. The way she protested death. Yearned for life when it was over.

I yearn for a different yarn. One that spits another tale. One where she was untroubled by reality.

By that, I mean I am troubled.

I yearn.

Beets

Yesterday I opened a can of beets from my mom's kitchen. I had a craving. Months ago my brother packed up her pantry goods and gave the box to me. I finally ate, stained my fingertips deep pink. I saved the juice—jarred up in my fridge. My mother's old juice sits stained with my grief.

Wound / Wound

I cut open / the gash

wound / between us

I did my best

to give her / something

pulled from / my heaving

to love her

unpick my / wound

wind me / respooled

With Thanks

Thank you to the Fine Arts Work Center, Provincetown, MA, Massachusetts Cultural Council, and Sundress Academy for the Arts for supporting my writing. Many thanks to the following workshop leaders: Kimiko Hahn, Jose Hernandez Diaz, Jane Huffman, Tatiana Johnson-Boria, Angela Siew, and Aimee Suzara.

Many thanks to the Emily Dickinson Museum for the opportunity to write in Emily's bedroom, "If Flowers Speak, or Victorian lore in a dead poet's room" was written in this sublime space.

Particular thanks to Jane Huffman, without her guidance, encouragement, and editor's eye, this book would not exist.

With deep appreciation for the caring support of hospice nurses, friends, and family, especially my brothers John, Alexander, and Maxwell.

Molly Akin lives on Cape Cod with her husband and two daughters. Molly is a 2023 recipient of a Massachusetts Cultural Council grant and her writing has been supported by the Sundress Academy for the Arts and Fine Arts Work Center. She has read in venues including the Emily Dickinson Museum, Fine Arts Work Center, Massachusetts Poetry Festival, New England Poetry Club, and What the Universe Is. Molly's work has recently been featured or is forthcoming from *Brevity, The Denver Quarterly, Identity Theory, Inflectionist Review, Moon City Review,* and *Paraselene. Hospice* is her first published collection.

.

www.ingramcontent.com/pod-product-compliance
Lightning Source LLC
Chambersburg PA
CBHW022056080426
42734CB00009B/1367